Happy Home Outside

Happy Home Outside

Everyday magic for outdoor life

Charlotte Hedeman Guéniau

First published in 2015 by
Jacqui Small LLP
74–77 White Lion Street
London N1 9PF

ISBN: 978 1 910254 11 0

A catalogue record for this book is
available from the British Library.

2017 2016 2015
10 9 8 7 6 5 4 3 2 1

Printed in China

Publisher Jacqui Small
Commissioning Editor Jo Copestick
Senior Editor Eszter Karpati
Designer Sarah Rock
Project Editor Sian Parkhouse
Production Maeve Healy

About the author Danish-born Charlotte
Hedeman Guéniau founded RICE in 1998,
a few months after her son Max was born.
Charlotte and her French husband Philippe
wanted to change their lives, having lived
and worked in Paris for 15 years, so they
moved to Odense, Denmark, and founded
their ethical homewares empire. Now, RICE
Denmark has a lovely office and showroom
in an old shipyard building near the
waterfront in Odense. The company employs
75 people internationally, and creates
influential homewares collections that are
ethically sourced and produced all over the
world. They are in stores from Liberty in
London to Illum in Copenhagen to Huset
in Malibu and So Perfect Eats in Denver,
USA. Charlotte is the author of the
bestselling *Happy Home* and several
other Danish cookery books. She blogs at
everydaymagic.dk.

CONTENTS

Foreword

As I write I'm fortunate enough to be spending a week on the African island of Mauritius. It has been a welcome reminder of how much I enjoy being outdoors. From biking through sugar cane fields with the wind rushing through my hair and sun heating the back of my neck, to hearing the clink of cutlery after sundown as people gather to share food and conversation with one another. To me, this is what the joy of being outdoors is all about – awakening the senses and spending time with loved ones, appreciating the quieter moments that life offers.

Outdoor spaces are an opportunity to reconnect with oneself and those around us; they offer a change in pace from the humdrum of day-to-day life. When we are outdoors we are more inclined to stop, to disconnect from our hurried, cluttered world and appreciate the simpler details and experiences. Through her new book, Charlotte shows how sharing special moments outdoors goes well beyond simply eating and drinking. Whether it's engaging in sporting activities, hosting a movie night or making pizza from scratch, Charlotte's simple yet imaginative ideas within these pages left me inspired to spend more time outdoors with those I love.

The benefits of such experiences are easy to see. As a teenager I would often spend a week of the summer holidays living with my gran in her thatched cottage, in the English countryside, and spend time helping her with projects in her traditional garden. These were treasured moments and memories were made for us both.

Why do I share these personal tales? Because by spending time together outdoors the experiences we earned brought my gran and I so much happiness. We seized the moment to spend time together outdoors to make something special, and whether you have a city balcony or a rolling country garden, you can do the same. Charlotte's easy yet stylish 'Happy Home Makes' and expert tips will give you a bounty of ideas to make the most of whatever you invest into your outdoor environment.

As I sat under a palm tree enjoying a traditional Mauritian lunch from a multi-coloured wicker basket – very similar to those sold by RICE – I realized how Charlotte and her team really do help others to embrace the everyday magic in life's experiences. To me there's no simpler, more rewarding magic than making memories outdoors with those you love. And there's no person better to show you how to do so in comfort and style than Charlotte. I hope you enjoy this delightful book, and all the outdoor memories you'll make from the ideas offered within its pages.

Will Taylor
www.brightbazaarblog.com
and author of *Bright.Bazaar: Embracing Colour for Make-You-Smile Style*

Opposite A lovely outdoor kitchen space – colourful and practical. This space would be ideal for parties and larger groups.

The Outdoor Life

Since writing *Happy Home: Everyday Magic for a Colourful Life*, two years have gone by. I had so much fun touring with the book – meeting customers and their customers, talking about everyday magic, chatting to lovely people who also believe in colours and their beauty and ability to lift and change moods and feelings. Now it is time to take the magic outside – to think about the life we live outdoors and the way we do it.

I get inspired when I am surrounded by beauty and colourful things, even in the simplest of ways. You could easily argue that there are bigger things to worry about in life than surrounding yourself with small ideas and colourful quirkiness, but little things count a great deal, too. My attitude is – why not? If you can bring a little everyday magic to things that matter to you, and if it can make you and the people who surround you smile, then go for it! I try to be optimistic for the world, and I always help wherever I can, both on a larger scale and in the small things. Can you recall that feeling of building a secret space under the dining room table – that cosy feeling of being in your own little world in there, hidden under a big blanket, lounging on lots of cushions with perhaps some biscuits and a great book? That exact feeling is the one I am chasing when I put up a canopy, when I go camping or when I pack to go on a shelter trip.

I am really excited to have some make-it-yourself projects in this book – simple ideas and easy tips on how to create items that again add fun, function and colour to your everyday lives. That is the essence of what we make at RICE. Our mantra is Live Love Laugh. Meeting with friends – living, loving, laughing together – is fuel for my soul. But more and more I feel the need to add something else other than just eat and drink and drink some more. Don't get me wrong, I am a huge fan of dinner parties, but sometimes I just like to add a bit of nuance to this. Hopefully you will feel inspired by the section on gatherings, the idea of meeting and doing things together, producing jam and chutney, baking, starting a book club or playing sports. It can all be combined with eating and drinking, but just adds extra value.

Enjoy, and stay happy outside in – and inside out.

Charlotte

Opposite Look on the bright side – sometimes my love goes to the brighter hues, and other times I am much more attracted to pastels and soft tones. I cannot really explain when or why, it just depends on my mood.

INSIDE OUT

Just breathe ... a bit of fresh air does wonders for the brain and the mental state. Every chance you get to be outside, you should grab it. 'Energy flows where attention goes' ... this is very true. So if you would like to use your outdoor space in a regular and more spontaneous way, pay some attention to how you can create a good set-up that enables you to live outdoors just as if it is a natural extension of the inside of your house.

Previous page Oh, to be part of the party around this balcony set-up – lovely teak furniture, great seating, comfort from soft cushions and cool drinks coming up ... simply summer at its best.

Opposite Marking a practical transition between inside and outside is lovely – a plastic carpet and a good doormat are the perfect solutions. You want those doors to be open and kids running in and out without necessarily bringing too much grass and dust along.

COLOURFUL COMFORT

Living easily both inside out and outside in is the perfect flow for me – I love to hang out in the fresh air, even if it's not always sunny with blue skies. And to make myself comfortable, I surround myself with cosiness and bright and cheerful accessories. In order for this to happen in a spontaneous and simple way you need to create practical and easy solutions, so you have ready or can carry all you need quickly and easily. When you decide you want to be outdoors, even on cooler days, it should not be such a big project you are put off the idea before you even begin.

I find that when you live in a country where the sun is not always your most trustworthy companion you need to be able to pick up and move quickly outside when the weather

Above Come rain or sunshine a plastic floor mat just looks great and you don't have to worry about bringing it in. Mixing bright fuchsia with green foliage is a feast for the eyes as well as for your feet.

Left and far left Flowers and a light make a very happy couple. Just keep it simple – one or two flowers is enough, especially when they are a contrasting colour to the vase.

Right There are no real rules, no recipes – everything is allowed. Mix without matching, floral prints, checked fabric and embroidery ... just play until you find something that works for your eyes.

allows it. I enjoy reading and lying outside, even in autumn, and in summer I love having dinner parties in the garden – entertaining outside often creates a more relaxed and easy-going atmosphere than a similar occasion held inside.

In Denmark we are sunseekers, and want to make the most of the summer sunshine when we are lucky enough to have it. In other countries you might seek the shade and nice cool areas. Whatever it is you need, you have to define it so you can organize yourself in a way for this to happen easily and smoothly. Do you need a sunshade, or a canopy to shelter under? Or some blankets to hand to ward off sudden breezes?

Below Girl meets house – glitter meets sequins; inside meets outside. Doormats and floor mats in the same hues make a visual flow from inside to outdoors.

Opposite Build a small cosy corner on your balcony – pull out the drinks cart and start out with a cup of tea and a good book. Later in the day you can build up to the evening with a refreshing sundowner ...

Above A few large cushions and a blanket and a corner with no wind and in the sun. If you have a spot like this, even the first spring days can be lovely and warm.

Opposite A foldable daybed and a small canopy made out of a few scarves that you tie together and you have a moveable luxury spot that you can plant anywhere – just follow the sun.

Try to plan your outdoor space in the same way you think about your interiors. In these pictures you can see that the balcony looks almost like a natural extension of the room. This is basically done by letting the same style continue through the doors and into the open. You can just as easily enjoy a drink inside as outside, and if you have friends who prefer the shade they can do that, without feeling excluded from the rest of the party. If you consider the outdoors as an extended part of your home, the transition from inside to outside should be quite smooth, both visually and practically, with something for everyone to enjoy.

Left A table for two please – just you and me, and with a view of the Eiffel Tower. Anything is possible with a little imagination.

Opposite I am happy to pull my dining room chairs outside from time to time – being comfortably seated is really crucial for me so I can properly relax.

COSY CORNERS EVERYWHERE ... CREATE THE SPACE FOR GREAT GATHERINGS AND MEMORABLE TIMES WITH FRIENDS OR JUST A MINDFUL MOMENT FOR YOURSELF

STRING CURTAINS

This is a combination of most of the things I love: **fun, colour** *and* **function**. *The curtains are bright and interesting to look at and make a visual airy separation instead of a real door. And don't forget – you'll have fewer insects in your house. There is something* **dreamy** *about string curtains – I am not sure why – but I love the feeling of going through one. We have made our very own fun version, put together with paper straws, melamine spoons and nice* **ribbons***, but you can buy curtains ready-made from plastic beads,* **string** *or strips of oilcloth.*

SPOON CURTAIN

This is easy to put together – get children involved if you can – and makes a great summer adornment.

YOU WILL NEED

* a bamboo rod
* lots of ribbons, string and lace trim
* 2 nails or hooks
* beads
* straws
* melamine spoons

HOW TO MAKE

Cut the bamboo rod a little wider than the door frame. Tie a ribbon at each end and hang the rod from 2 nails or hooks placed over the door. It is easier to start like this – then you have constant control on the overall look. Use a small stepladder if necessary to tie the strings on the rod. Remember to add extra length when cutting the strings and ribbons as knots consume quite a bit. Cut ribbons, strings and lace trim and decorate some with beads and pieces of straws; tie melamine spoons on others. Spread out the spoons and avoid clusters of one colour.

SUMMER ROOM

Setting up an outside room for summer is wonderful and a must in my world. Most people I know prefer to spend as much time outside as possible, and I firmly believe that everything feels better, tastes better and looks better when you are outside. It is incredible how much a little fresh air and a few rays affect our moods. Your outdoor summer room should be very much you! Let it reflect your personal style and it will feel and look like a natural extension of your home.

Comfortable seating is crucial and outside hang-outs tend to be on the softer seating side and require plenty of textiles. Quilts, cushions, throws, bolsters – you name it.

Opposite and left Clean lines – yet colourful in a classy way. Mixing black and white with colours is quite the clever match – remember it does not have to be either/or when it comes to colour.

Above Increase your living space by just opening the door and stepping straight into an exquisite outdoor summer room, complete with floor mats, soft seating and a similar colour scheme.

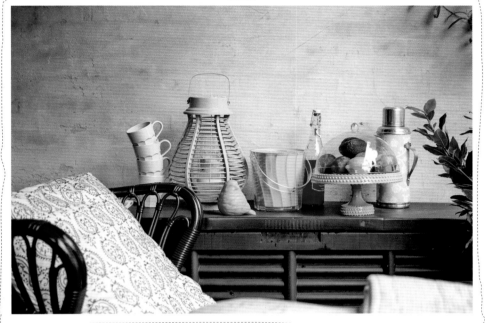

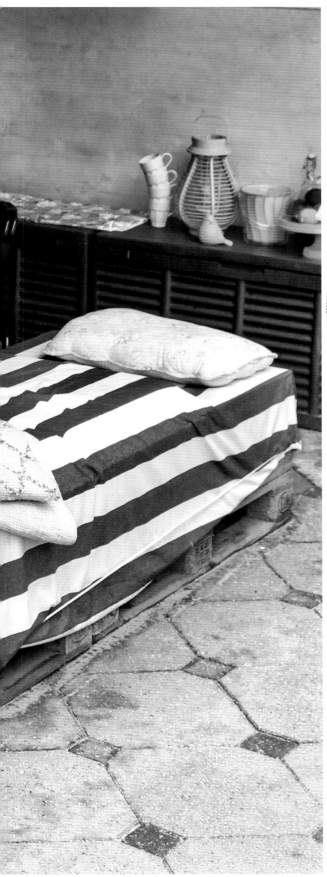

This is when a canopy comes in handy. Not only will it provide shade during the hottest hours of the day, it will also protect you from the rain. It also means you can leave your cushions and blankets outside for the night without worrying that they will get wet or ruined.

If you don't have a canopy, make sure to keep some big baskets or boxes ready for storage. It can be a bit tedious if you have to carry everything in and out all the time and most likely you will end up spending less time outside, because you can't really be bothered to do so. I mean – let's be honest here. No one wants it to be a huge project to enjoy a few hours in the sun. It should be easy – just like walking from one room to another. Put in the final touches with lots of lanterns, lovely flowers and anything else you feel is essential for you to feel comfortable and at home.

Left and above A table, a chair and a few pallets, plus lots of textiles for soft furnishing, and you have a cosy-looking haven. Keep all essentials ready at hand, so you don't have to run from one end of the house to the other.

HERB GARDEN

I beg your pardon ... I never promised you a herb garden. When we first moved to Denmark we lived in the countryside and I had this big romantic dream of a vegetable garden, being almost self-sufficient, harvesting every night with my happy children. I did have a few Kodak moments with them pulling up carrots and beetroots while they were screaming with joy, and I have to say they were so enthusiastic about the vegetables that they ate every mouthful. But then we went on holiday and when we came home everything was dead. I repeated the scenario for two years and then accepted that perhaps later in my life I will have time to water my plants and be more organized!

I have become less ambitious with my romantic food dreams since then, but I do love that feeling of harvesting. So a herb garden is the answer for me. All you need is a small table and a few pots and you can easily make your own little herb 'field'. There is an enormous satisfaction attached to collecting crops for your dinner ... even if it is just herbs. Fresh herbs taste wonderful, too, so you will find that having a nice variety of herbs to plunder is highly addictive.

Left Keep a pair of scissors attached to the table so it's always easy to cut the herbs you want. Easy access is the key to frequent use ... and you can never really have too many herbs.

Opposite Mix and match all kinds of flowerpots for a personal look. Some herbs require more room than others, so remember to use pots in sizes that fit. And remember, for herbs in pots, water is life.

PLANTING CONTAINERS

You can do a lot with colourful planting containers. I find that most materials only last for a short while outside anyway. I don't really mind if my **baskets** *don't last forever so I sometimes choose to use colourful* **raffia** *baskets. I love mixing materials in my planters as well.* **Metal***, rattan,* **plastic, ceramic** *– but of course preferably colourful. If you want to build a small* **divider** *partition you can plant* **bamboo** *in baskets. That way they don't invade your entire space. We have actually cut holes in the bottom of ours so they have their roots in the ground and we don't worry about watering, but at the same time they stay in a controlled area.*

THE RULE IS THERE ARE NO RULES WHEN IT COMES TO PLANTING. USE BASKETS AND POTS IN MIXED MATERIALS – SO MUCH MORE JOYFUL TO LOOK AT

PLANTS AND FLOWERS
REALLY GROW ON
YOU ...

HAPPY HOME
MAKE!

FLOWERPOTS

*We have a weakness for flowerpots –
these pots are easy to customize and you
will feel like a talented do-it-yourself
queen once you have made these ...*

YOU WILL NEED
* old flowerpots
* water-based or wood paint
* ribbons/string/fabric for decoration

HOW TO MAKE
Paint simple borders at the top of flower
pots. A few gold details on the painted
borders add a little elegance to the overall
look. Tie a length of ribbon or fabric
around the top of the flowerpots once
they are dry. We have used water-based
hobby paint and some leftover wood/
metal paint.

FLOWER BOXES

*Make sweet flower boxes from old wooden
crates. Create a look of irregularity –
avoid making it look too finished.*

YOU WILL NEED
* wooden crates
* old table legs
* screws
* paint

HOW TO MAKE
Use screws to attach the table legs,
screwing down through the base of the
crate. Paint some crates and for others
paint just the legs – especially if you have
found a particularly nice crate. Sometimes
just a gold detail is enough.

HAPPY HOME
MAKE!

SMOOTH TRANSITIONS

Keep everything you need for outdoor living ready to go in big baskets so you can jump out the door and set up camp the second you feel like it. And just as easily and swiftly pack it up if the weather turns or you just want to go inside again. Keeping it in a basket just inside the door makes it easily available at all times, without looking messy.

Sometimes it is all about seizing the moment, and there's not much seizing anything if you need to spend hours gathering up the things you need to create your own personal oasis. A good basic outdoor kit could be a few blankets and throws, and cushions in all shapes and sizes. Good floor mats will keep the dirt and grass at bay. Keep vases and flowers within close reach, too – it is all about the little details. Include a pretty tablecloth if you need, or just want, one, with a few pegs (pins) to keep it under control. And candles and lanterns are always a great idea. And voila! You are all set for a great time.

Opposite Marking a beautiful and logical transition – style and comfort inside out and outside in.

Right A large basket filled with cushions and blankets ready to go ... and at the same time it looks quite cosy and cool even when waiting to be grabbed up and transported outside.

Above and right A beautiful tablecloth can brighten up the dullest of tables. With a few quirky clothes pegs (pins) at the corners it is kept under control if the wind picks up.

MIXING A BIT OF BLACK AND WHITE WITH PASTEL PINKS MAKES FOR A SHARPER AND LESS ROMANTIC LOOK

BARBECUE BASICS

Nothing signals relaxed, casual fun like a good old barbecue. It does not require a lot of preparation, and there's nothing more summery and mouthwatering than the delicious smell, seeping through the air. This is a gathering where nobody necessarily sits down at the table and eats at the same time – the kids can roam freely in the garden and just grab a sausage or a drumstick when hungry. This is also the perfect base for a 'everybody-brings-a-salad-or-bread-or-other-side-dish' get-together, where you will only be in charge of the meat and drinks. Or people can bring their own meat and you take care of the salads and side dishes. Do you want a designated barbecue-master to be in charge of the barbecue all night? Or do you just want people to grill their own meat? Anything goes. This is not the kind of event where formal etiquette is upheld, it is all about spending some very relaxed hours in good company. Good people, good food and great drinks – that is the recipe for success.

Opposite Keep eyesores out of sight in fun, practical ways. Stow away the gas canister you use for your barbecue in a colourful basket.

Below left and right Get it all lined up ready to chop. If you do not have running water nearby it's a good idea to fill a bowl or a bucket with water so you don't need to leave your work station all the time.

Right The simplest set-up ever – a small table and a barbecue – and voilà, your outdoor kitchen is up and running. And remember – barbecuing is not only for summertime! It tastes equally good on a snowy winter day.

SEATING

*Grab a seat! Mix materials and throw a **cushion** on top. Bamboo furniture looks great, and has that **retro cosiness** about it, but can sometimes be a bit fragile when left in the rain for too long. I don't mind a bit of a weather-beaten look, but if you are not comfortable with that, you should go for **powder-coated metal** options or plastic. Always add some rugs or cushions for a soft seat so your bare summer legs don't get hurt.*

OUTDOOR FURNITURE WITH VERY DIFFERENT LOOKS AND DIFFERENT STYLES – THE CHOICE IS YOURS

PAINT A FEW PALLETS, TOP THEM OFF WITH A
MATTRESS AND SOME COMFY CUSHIONS AND
YOU HAVE A LOVELY DAYBED IN NO TIME

CUSHIONS & THROWS

I have a **soft spot** *for throws and cushions. And you can never have too many: hand-embroidered cushions for their sheer beauty;* **round velvet poufs** *or* **floor cushions** *come in handy when multiple guests shows up;* **crochet throws** *to chase the chill away; square* **statement pillows** *for your bold days; and chair cushions double function as back supports when tied to the top rail of a bench – the options are endless and I love them all!*

A SHEEPSKIN IS SO SOFT TO SIT ON AND WELL SUITED FOR THE EARLY DAYS OF THE SEASON WHEN THE AIR MIGHT STILL BE A BIT CHILLY

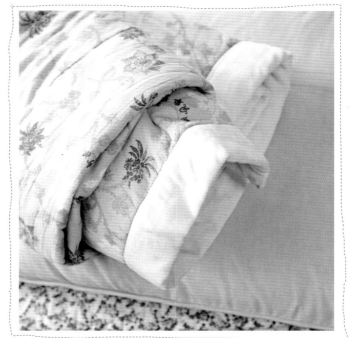

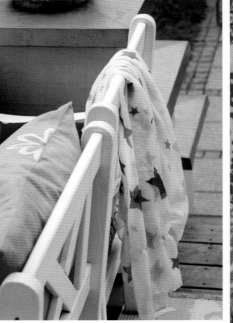

HAPPY HOME MAKE!

TEA TOWEL CUSHION

This tea (dish) towel had a pompom border, but you can add it yourself.

YOU WILL NEED

* a tea (dish) towel
* scraps of fabric and embroidery
* filler/pad according to cushion cover size
* pompom ribbon, if you like
* zip, if you like

HOW TO MAKE

Take a pretty tea towel and fold it in half. Add some fabric and embroidery pieces to the part that will be on the front. Stitch the sides and put in the filler or pad. Stitch the final seam or sew in a zip for easy maintenance.

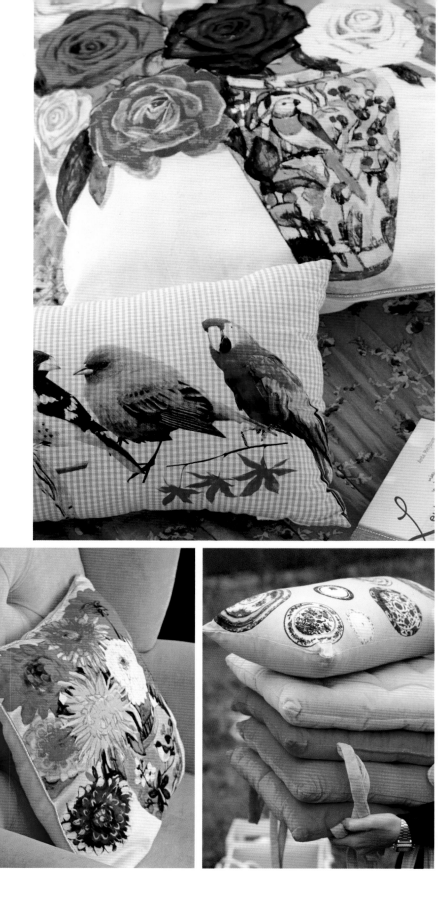

Left Always look on the bright side - add plenty of zingy colour and a few upbeat slogans, then just enjoy the mix and match of all the vivid hues you can muster.

Opposite Give your old couch a new dress each season - a few blankets and some cushions and it is a whole different story.

PEACE AND LOVE AND ALL THINGS HAPPY – WHO COULDN'T FAIL TO FEEL CHEERFUL WHEN SURROUNDED BY SUCH A VIBRANT ARRAY?

OUTDOOR ROOMS

I am not sure why, but small outdoor rooms – winter gardens, huts, greenhouses, you name it – have always appealed to me. Perhaps it is that feeling of being in a small cosy space, like when you were a child building a hideaway world under a table covered with a blanket. A mini summer house that you open up when days get warmer and longer – it does not need to be heated – has exactly that attractive and rather romantic feel to it.

Previous page Spaces that you use on special occasions or when you are just alone or with a friend or spaces you only use in summer or on certain days – I believe they do something to our state of mind. We are more present and appreciative, and perhaps that is also what appeals to me.

Opposite The soft green colour of this little garden house or pavilion is calming and poetic. It is very Gustavian in feel, very Scandinavian summer.

This page Inside the pavilion, keep it airy and light in style– give the feeling of calmness, of wanting to sit with a cup of tea and a book. Perhaps later in the day you might be joined by a friend as well.

WELCOME IN

What a perfect hideaway this is. It's somewhere to escape to in all sorts of weather. On sunny days throw the doors open and let the sun shine right in. On cooler days it will still provide a welcoming shelter – a place to hide from the worst of the elements while still enjoying a feeling of being surrounded by nature. Pick out some elegant furniture with good shapes that will help to give you a feeling of gracious living. And let the garden begin on the stairs to tempt you in. Add pots of greenery and add in seasonal boosts of brightly coloured flowers. You can use a pavilion like this as a private retreat, bringing along a book or even a laptop to catch up on some online browsing. If you are feeling more sociable, invite a friend along – settle in and set the world to rights.

This page Bigger is not always better. Fitted with a mini kitchen and a bed, a small garden sanctuary like this can double as a guest house, too, when needed.

THIS IS THE CUTEST GARDEN HOUSE EVER –
WHEN YOU WALK INTO THIS SPACE IT FEELS
LIKE YOU ARE STEPPING INTO A CHILDHOOD
DREAM OR THE PAGES OF A QUIRKY BOOK

Left Create a nice transition inside out and outside in – this greenhouse is built on part of a wooden deck, which also means the cold and humidity from the ground is less of a problem.

Below Find an old bench with a compartment under the seat. You can use it for storing games and cards. Keeping these things close by means you play more often and spontaneously.

Opposite A big old wicker basket for storing extra blankets and cushions keeps them from fading from the sunlight. Having blankets to hand makes it more comfortable to linger outside, even on a chilly autumn day. Just hug yourself in a cosy blanket and enjoy.

GREENHOUSE GETAWAY

A small greenhouse is a great way to expand your outdoor living space. This is particularly appealing if you live in a country where the weather is not always on the sunny side. It prolongs the stay-outside season by quite a bit, and is a great way to spend time feeling like you are outdoors. It's a good idea to keep a light outdoorsy style to the furniture – something that is robust and doesn't require a lot of maintenance. It is also nice to keep board games, cards, paper and things to be creative with ready to hand – this makes it easy to do something together, as a family. You can perhaps recreate that feeling of having time to while away in the endless summers of your youth, and increase the ability to always stay playful in every way. Sometimes spending time in just a few square metres gives a feeling of closeness and great family moments – like small bite-sized tastes of camping with the informal and relaxed atmosphere that can create. Inside is outside and outside easily becomes inside.

RESIST THE TEMPTATION TO USE YOUR GREENHOUSE AS A DUMPING GROUND FOR GARDEN TOOLS. ALWAYS KEEP IT TIDY, JUST LIKE A LIVING ROOM INSIDE YOUR HOUSE, SO IT WILL BE EASY TO LIVE IN

Right and below My friend uses her gorgeous greenhouse both as an office and a dining room. She positioned the greenhouse on a piece of land where she was building a new house and she used it a lot, even during autumn and winter.

AN OUTDOOR SANCTUARY - EVEN WHEN THE WIND IS COLD. A FEW RAYS OF SUNSHINE ALLOWS YOUR OUTDOOR SPACE TO BE LIVED IN

PAINTED
SODA BOTTLES

*I love the shape of old glass soda
bottles and they look great in a group
with single flowers in them.*

YOU WILL NEED
✱ old soda bottles
✱ water-based hobby paint -
   remember to pick some gold

HOW TO MAKE
Paint simple borders, words, berries
or flower buds on old glass soda
bottles. Add a few gold details for a
more elegant look.

OUTDOOR KITCHEN

An outdoor kitchen is a haven. It doesn't have to be complicated at all – just a simple roof built out from your garage or the side of the house will do. All meals can be eaten outside if you have a roof over your head to keep you dry at all times. One electric cooking plate or a barbecue is all you need to get started. It's a good idea to stock up on cups and plates and everything else you need to set a table, so you don't have to run inside all the time. Keep a few pots and pans to hand as well.

That first dinner to open the summer season is so special – and moments spent like this are the ones you remember when autumn and winter hit you. One summer we just put up a big pavilion on our terrace and we spent so much time outside – we managed to create a holiday feeling, playing cards and board

Previous page With a roof over your head, an extra outdoor room is useable in all kinds of weather. And it is a special feeling to eat pancakes or just drink coffee while the rain is drumming on the roof.

Left and above Lovely pastels, plastic and wood: mix and match materials for that relaxed and carefree look.

Opposite All the bare necessities for cooking a great meal are right at hand. Make it easy and enjoyable to use your outdoor kitchen regularly.

COLOUR ME HAPPY ... TRY GARDEN PLANTERS WITH FLOWERS ON THE WALL, FUNNY LITTLE SIGNS OR POSTERS

games even if it was raining. We have very sweet memories from that summer so we are now planning to build a more permanent solution in glass. A good way to try out this idea is to put up a tent.

When stocking up your outdoor kitchen, think low maintenance. Use durable materials that can stand the weather changes. Melamine, plastic and treated wood are all good. Then you don't have to take everything inside all the time, but can just leave it out until the season is over. Airtight tins are great for spices, coffee and tea. Lanterns for candles create a cosy light when dusk sets in. Being outside means you have the opportunity to go a bit crazier when decorating than you would inside. Pick the brightest plates and the funkiest prints.

This page A coffee maker is a great gadget for your outdoor kitchen. It is all about easy access to everything. The less you need to fetch things from inside the house, the more natural and relaxed the outdoor kitchen will feel.

FUNKY SHELTER

Create an extra room in your garden. My friend bought a simple (and not very nice) metal shelter from a hardware store and turned it into a fabulous guest house/extra teenage space/lounge area. So the shelter would sit more naturally in the environment, she covered it with barked poles on the outside and planks on the inside, and suddenly she had the coolest shelter that just blends in. Another great idea was building a small porch or decking area at the front of it, just using three pallets. I love pallets, they are the best – the cheapest recycled piece of wood ever. Only your imagination limits the ideas for multipurpose usage. Like here – a small veranda – or as a couch, a lounge chair, a swing or stack them on top of each other and use them for shelves for storing apples outside, you name it ... See pages 102–3 for a nice and very easy-to-make pallet swing.

This page An affordable way to add an extra room to your house – this is ideal as a guest room as it will lend a little privacy to the inhabitant. A makeshift couch/bed, a small bedside table and a nice chair to sit in and the room is ready for visitors.

Opposite The way this shelter has been dressed with wood on all outside walls makes it disappear into the surroundings nicely. The little porch invites you to stay outside and enjoy the garden life.

HAPPY HOME MAKE!

STORAGE POUCHES

Gather these pretty fabric bags on a bamboo cane or peg rail. Tie a long piece of ribbon or string at each end of the cane for hanging.

YOU WILL NEED
* fabric leftovers
* doilies, crochet work and pompom ribbon
* string, tape or cord
* peg rail/bamboo cane

HOW TO MAKE
Sew fabric pouches and thread a drawstring through a narrow casing at the top. Decorate with old doilies, crochet pieces and pompom ribbons.

This page Make a funky decorative garland out of old crocheted doilies, glittery toys and whatever else you have around your house ... exercise your imagination to set the scene.

TO HAVE AND TO HOLD ...

As much as I love decorating my outdoor space with **loads of cushions and blankets***, mattresses and so on, I resent the mess it makes and the time it consumes when you have to carry everything inside every evening. Creating* **outdoor storage options** *is a must. Separate the two worlds and you avoid the big mess inside every evening or rainy day. When you have no other option but to store inside,* **invest in beautiful baskets** *or wooden boxes and* **trunks** *that you enjoy looking at. Baskets are easy to carry around and if they have a lid, you can even use them as side tables.*

LIVING IN A BOX CAN BE AN ATTRACTIVE IDEA AFTER ALL IF YOU GO ABOUT IT THE RIGHT WAY ...

UPLIFTING SLOGANS

Make a bold statement with washi tape for the world to see.

YOU WILL NEED
* spools of different washi tape
* assorted stickers

HOW TO MAKE
Think of a positive and uplifting thought. Using a combination of lengths of tape and stickers, make the slogan on the inside of the lid of a storage box. It will cheer you up every time you open it.

HAPPY HOME
MAKE!

CAMPING OUT

If you are lucky enough to live in a country where you can find public nature shelters you should really grab the opportunity and organize a big gathering with friends and family. Everyone brings mattresses, cushions, blankets, sleeping bags and lanterns and in no time you will have the cosiest shelter, where you just feel like climbing in, curling up under a blanket and waiting for someone to read you a story. If you are a bit adventurous you can sleep in these shelters all year round. But a fun gathering could be to go at a time when the forest is full of mushrooms, and you could all go on a mushroom hunt – foraging for dinner (see pages 139–40). Make a big fireplace and just cook away under the stars.

Left and above For me, the devil is in the detail – I love to bring banners and colourful things to make the atmosphere even more personal.

IT DOESN'T TAKE MUCH: A MATTRESS, A FEW BLANKETS, SOME CUSHIONS AND SOME CANDLES, AN OUTDOOR SHELTER AND BINGO. MY DREAMS ARE ALREADY STARTING ...

Left Hang fabric bags on convenient hooks around the walls and you can keep clutter off the floor.

Opposite Keep it bright and remember a touch of humour. I love these poodle cushions – they always make me smile.

MAGICAL TREEHOUSE

A little fairy-tale treehouse must be everybody's dream. I know it is mine. Imagine being in that house hidden from the rest of the world, listening to the birds and the wind rustling the leaves. Trees have a certain energy – some people even like to hug them. I always feel grounded and very centred when I am surrounded by trees, and to have a small wooden house in the top of an old tree must be magical. My garden does not have a tree like this, but if yours does then I hope to inspire you to design your own little shelter in the air. You do not need much – some wood and perhaps some recycled windows, and maybe a few hours of skilled carpentry help, unless you have smarter hands than I do.

Opposite When you see this wonderful treehouse you can almost imagine the stories that have been told – the books, the thoughts and dreams that have flown around this space.

Left and above And as always, lots of cushions and blankets and a good soft mattress and all is well in the world …

USING MASKING TAPE OR FLUORESCENT STARS TO CREATE A MOOD OF HAPPINESS AND TO SPUR THE IMAGINATION IS A GREAT WAY TO DECORATE THE WALLS INSIDE THE HOUSE

PICK A BUNCH OF GREENERY, BERRIES AND FLOWERS TO BRING THE GARDEN RIGHT INSIDE

Opposite and below A treehouse represents everything cosy and good for me – a place to read, eat, talk, tell secrets, a place to plot and plan and dream big, or perhaps read aloud with a friend, or just take an afternoon nap.

Above and right Large glass doors open to the hexagonal interior of this most beautiful tea pavilion. The salmon and lime painted walls with the green borders arching towards the high ceiling gives a very Jane Austen feel to the entire room. It's perfect for a ladies' lounge or book club meeting.

Opposite Comfortable seating for all sets a relaxed yet slightly romantic backdrop for an evening of thoughtful talk and laughter.

THE BEAUTIFUL BOOK CLUB

This garden pavilion is one amazing shelter – not many of us are lucky enough to have a hideaway like this in our garden. But setting up a book club is something we can all do. It is a very nice way to gather friends and *do* something together. Something that inspires and pushes you to think and express thoughts on what you have read – which for me is something I rarely do. I usually read and keep it to myself. Meet up with your friends perhaps every second month. Create a space where everyone has a good seat, a nice blanket, and where everybody can see each other. Perhaps the host can also manage the talking, to make sure everyone gets a word in. An idea could be to prepare a few questions in advance, to see what your friends think about a certain character or a specific chapter in the book – these talks often lead to other places.

Perhaps a light meal should be served – you could even theme it according to the book. Imagine drinking whisky and talking about a book whose story took place in the Scottish highlands. Or eating the hottest curry ever while you discuss that Indian story. If you were to invite me, I'd say yes with the biggest smile on my face!

RELAXING OUTDOORS

Let's hang out ... If you work on creating a great life in your garden or on your veranda, putting the same kind of effort into your outer space as you do into interior decorating, you will surely find you spend much more time, and much more enjoyable time, outside. Years ago we invested in some amazing couches. Woven in plastic, they can stay outside all year. It has turned out to be the best buy ever. They demand no maintenance, paint or other hard work, so just suit our lives.

Previous page This is such a welcoming corner in the garden. The floor slabs and large potted olive trees clearly frame the space and make it feel like a room.

Opposite Make your couches so inviting that you just want to settle in. Mix all you have – cushions and blankets – and style it as if it was inside your living room.

HANGING OUT

We spend a lot of time in our garden so having the right furniture is important. We lie down, read, chill and just enjoy. And when we have guests we can all be comfortably seated – just as if we were hanging out inside the house.

It is so much nicer to be comfortably seated and it means you stay longer outside, and fully enjoy the seasons. Often we enjoy a pleasant dinner in the garden, seated at the dining table, and afterwards we prepare seats and blankets for everybody to sit comfortably and warm. Scandinavian summer nights can get very humid when the dew is falling and the temperature drops rapidly once the sun has disappeared. But having kitted ourselves out with everything we need, and with drinks to hand, we can stay out as long as we want and are not chased in by the increasing chill.

Left Colourful acrylic glasses are perfect for outdoor parties. They are easy on the eye and you don't have to worry about broken glass.

Below left and right Create different areas for people to gather together and relax, and include soft seating and a table positioned conveniently close to set a drink down. What more could you need?

AS DUSK
SETTLES THE
PARTY IS JUST
BEGINNING ...

On quiet, starry summer nights my daughter and I sometimes opt to spend the whole night under the stars on our comfortable couches. Such cosy moments ...

When we are making more of a party of it and inviting more people, it's still important to create lots of perching points and places where people can gather comfortably in sociable groups. Having lots of small tables gives lots of flexibility. Guests can set down plates of food and drinks, and if the tables are lightweight they can be moved around as people need.

I like to think of myself as not being a perfectionist, as this has quite a negative and limiting ring to my ears, but I am a person with a strong eye for aesthetics. Wherever I am, I create small colourful spaces; it matters to me that the things I surround myself with in my everyday life are things that make my eyes happy ... and if my eyes are happy my heart sings. Perhaps you could argue that this is a bit superficial and shallow – but that is how it works for me.

Opposite and this page
When hosting a party I love to use tall cocktail tables – they help ensure a very relaxed and loose atmosphere, plus they make it easy for everyone to mingle freely. No one is stuck at a table and the energy flows more smoothly. They require minimum effort when it comes to table setting – just a flower and some light and you are all set.

Left How very decadent. Cut a branch full of ripe apples, put it in a vase and let people pick their own snack right from the source. Talk about fresh produce ...

Above A small moveable table is an essential item for your outdoor life. It is easy to move around and provides a steady surface for you to put your drinks on.

Opposite Nothing left to do but lie down and count the stars and perhaps your blessings as well. Or maybe curl up with a friend, for a nice chat and good laughs. A cute garden gnome hidden in the bamboo partition follows the activities.

COSY CORNERS

Creating small self-contained worlds wherever possible can become a hobby, and you really feel like you are in a world of your own when nestled into this kind of covered seating. Find your favourite corner in the garden and set up the seating. Create the illusion of a defined space by placing a floor mat on the ground and a table within reach. Now you have your own undisturbed and very cosy corner. I find that when you cover the seats of your furniture with soft blankets it gives the feeling of a cosy daybed, and at the same time it is very practical as you can easily wash and change the blankets whenever needed, or if you just fancy a new colour scheme.

SERVING UP A TREAT

*I had this very cute book when I was a child about Amalie – her mum always prepared **amazing** trays for her, with a small flower, a nice **napkin**, homemade bread and jam. I think this is where my attachment to life on trays started. You can really create a **small universe** on very few square inches; the 'good morning, have a **lovely day**' tray. The 'heyyy it's time for drinks' tray. The 'let's read and have a nice cup of tea and some forbidden chocolate' tray. The 'shots **shots** shots shots' tray or the TV dinner tray … It's up to you to decide what you are up for, and then create trays for yourself or your friends.*

A TRAY FOR EVERY OCCASION: TEA, WINE, DRINKS, AFTERNOON SNACKS … A WORLD OF LOVE ON A PLATTER

CREATING A LITTLE WORLD ON A TRAY ... IT DOESN'T TAKE MUCH BUT IT BRINGS A LOT OF JOY

Stick some legs on an old drawer and paint it ... this is a great idea for a small table that can be used inside and outside. You can make a whole bunch with legs in varying lengths and use them as flower stands, end tables or snack trays. Put a cushion on top of a low variety and you have a nice footrest as well. Just make sure the legs on each table are even or your table will wobble.

DRAW THE LINE WITH THIS FANCY BUT SIMPLE UPCYCLING IDEA

DRAWER TABLE

Make a fun, small end table from an old drawer and second-hand table legs.

YOU WILL NEED
* wooden drawer
* old table legs
* screws
* paint

HOW TO MAKE
The legs can be sawn into several pieces, so you will have legs for both a table and the flower boxes (see page 33). Screw them into place through the base of the drawer. Paint the finished table in a funky colour.

LAZY LOUNGING

I just love to lounge around on a big beautiful quilt placed straight on the grass. On hot summer days the grass has a particular smell that takes me right back to my childhood, where the summers were always sunny, the sky always blue and the ice creams much bigger … at least that's how I remember it. But to lie on a quilt with plenty of cushions – reading books, writing a diary or just dozing off, looking through the branches of a tree and just doing absolutely nothing, while your mind wanders – is amazing. We should all indulge in a few hours of luxurious laziness once in a while. One of the best features about the quilt is that it is the easiest thing to move around the garden, so you always lie in your favourite spot, whether that's sun or shade.

This page and opposite Inside my house the easiest way to restyle and change things around is with cushions and it's the same outdoors – and do they come in handy when trying to create that perfectly comfortable lying/sitting position …

DOGS ALWAYS FIND THE PERFECT SPOT IN A GARDEN. FOLLOW THEIR EXAMPLE – GRAB A QUILT AND JUST PICK UP AND GO

COOL CANOPY

A canopy serves multiple purposes. It provides shade from the sun and shelter from the rain, but it also gives an enclosed feeling, which can be nice if you are a larger party and like to keep people gathered. Canopies come in a vast variety of shapes and sizes. They can be for one person, or big enough to cover an entire party. But you can also create your own and very personal version from a few easy-to-find things (see opposite) and nestle into your own private world among the trees. There is something magical and luxurious about lying under a lovely canopy, lounging on lovely quilts and mountains of pillows ... dozing off or reading a book. The sun filters through in such a pretty way, creating a play of light and shade that changes through the day.

CANOPY

YOU WILL NEED

* 4 bamboo canes diameter 2cm (1 inch)
* 2 tablecloths, or fabric according to the canopy size you want
* flag rope
* 2 spears from tent poles
* 2 tent pegs
* a saw and drill

HOW TO MAKE

Stitch the length of the tablecloths together and make casings about 10cm (4 inches) wide at both ends. If you want a border on the canopy like we have made, add it after making the casing. Saw 2 canes to a length about 10cm (4 inches) wider than the width of the fabric. Drill a hole through the ends of both canes.

Saw the remaining 2 rods according to the height you want – my recommended height is 2m (6½ feet). Saw between the nodes to make sure that the canes are hollow. Attach the 2 spears at the top.

Insert a cane with holes into one of the casings and pull flag rope through the hole at one side. Tie it with a sturdy knot. Run rope around a tree or pole about 20cm (8 inches) higher than the front poles, then tie it through the hole at the other end of the cane.

Insert a cane with holes into the other casing and put the spears through the holes. Add a long piece of flag rope at the top of each spear (these will work as guy ropes) and hoist the poles. Tie the ends of the 2 flag ropes to the pegs and secure them in the ground. Adjust the 2 poles so they are straight and the guy ropes are taut.

HAPPY HOME
MAKE!

COMFORTABLE COUCHES

When it comes to pure relaxation, comfort is key! I am personally almost unable to sit upright in a couch – five seconds after sitting down, my **feet are up** *and I am more laying than sitting. Pick good furniture for your cosy corners. Try it out to make sure that you can really* **relax** *in it. You can't properly relax with a spring*

digging into your leg or a sharp edge wedging your rib. **Blankets** *and* **cushions** *are a given, of course ... and you cannot have too many. A daybed or a* **garden swing** *are great alternatives to the more ordinary couch and they make great welcoming spots around the garden. Ohh to be outside – even when night falls and it gets a bit cooler you can* **snuggle** *up in a beautiful hand-crocheted blanket. Yes please, is my answer.*

A THOUSAND WAYS TO SOFTEN UP ...
CUSHIONS AND BLANKETS ALWAYS HELP
YOU IN THAT DIRECTION

NO MATTER YOUR AGE A SWING IS ALWAYS ATTRACTIVE. PERHAPS IT'S THE FEELING OF BEING A BABY AGAIN THAT APPEALS ... WHO KNOWS? JUST GET INTO THE SWING OF THINGS AND ENJOY

PALLET SWING

This swing is wide enough for one to stretch out or for two to share.

YOU WILL NEED
* a pallet painted a cheerful colour
* 2 lengths of strong rope
* duct tape
* 2 strong metal pulley clips with a rope loop

HOW TO MAKE
Drill a hole big enough for the rope in all four corners of the bottom boards. Pull the ropes through and tie knots, securing the ends with duct tape to prevent unravelling. Finally, hang your swing from some strong branches.

HAPPY HOME
MAKE!

OUTDOOR ENTERTAINING

Enjoying a meal together in a relaxed ambience – surrounded by good people – is part of the most joyful everyday magic moments in my life. It might sound shallow and a bit odd but I really have difficulties striking up a deeper friendship with people who do not enjoy good food and good wine ... eating together is a special and quite intimate moment. You share a meal and a part of your life, while hopefully enjoying each other's company at the same time.

Previous page Living outside is easy – mix and match old and new; keep it practical, fun and functional.

Opposite Setting the scene is an important part of the outcome you wish for: an informal table setting perfectly suits a relaxed and chilled atmosphere.

PIZZA PARTY

When you are a big group of people and, in particular, a group of all ages, it's fun to have a do-it-yourself dinner party. It creates a loose, happy and slightly hectic atmosphere that you just have to embrace ...

Small children are hard to keep focused – even if you all sit properly at the table parents are often running around after their small kids, who have no patience to sit. The older teenagers usually just want to eat and then

Left and above My favourite kind of table is long and full of friends of all ages. These ingredients will always be uppermost in my mind. And then come the fun extras ... such as a table set with love, flowers and colourful plates. Involve your guests in the preparations – get them to hang up the lanterns in the trees. Everybody is happy to help.

seek their own corners as soon as possible. So with a mixed crowd like this it can be a good idea to create a build-your-own dinner. These meals demand a bit of preparation beforehand, but once guests have arrived – and you put everything on the table – the dice are thrown and you have the chance to just join the party and blend in with your friends.

I have held quite a few pizza nights since my kids were little. We sometimes held pizza competitions as well – where everybody explained what they had tried to make and why. Like my friend who had dropped his pizza and claimed the reason for the lack of topping was that he tried to illustrate the world and parts of it without any food and other parts with too much food. We would all give points for taste, appearance and so on. And magically, when I added up the points, the kids were always the winners. My kids are bigger now, and do not fall for this kind of point system anymore. But pizza is always popular, especially among their friends.

I love this relaxed and informal atmosphere – you get the chance to talk and mingle and have a drink while you are waiting for your turn. Some might need a bit of guidance as to how to construct the best pizza, the right one that just fits their taste. You can also step in to speed up the process a little. If you grab the role of the one who ensures a smooth and speedy cooking process, it can get a bit hot around the fire, but still fun and light-hearted.

Right Paper fans dangling from the branches, colourful strings of lights, mix-and-match chairs and tables – it's very much about the love and care that is put into the setting.

I prepare the pizza dough in advance, and the tomato purée mix, plus of course chop, slice and dice every topping I know will be popular. I mix a garlic oil and some chilli oil – just ready to be drizzled on the crispy warm pizza. It's a really good idea to buy some real pizza stones and put them inside your barbecue so you get really hot temperatures and are able to obtain a great crispy result.

You must understand and enjoy that this kind of evening is rather chaotic and messy. No one really eats at the same time – only two pizzas are ready simultaneously. If you are willing to share you can cut them in small bite sizes and do that. If not, you eat in turns. Some people just want their very own personal pizza.

Once the kids are done making their pizzas I usually make a few for sharing – this ensures that we all get a bit of food inside our stomachs, and do not just survive on wine.

Left Personally, I see details, I enjoy them – I love it. But I know a lot of people who don't really keep their eyes open. A plate with birds, a lovely tablecloth, colourful napkins, funky acrylic glasses ... and you have my full attention.

Opposite Pizza nights are the best – messy, loud and crazy kind of nights. You need baking (parchment) paper to slide the pizzas onto the barbecue, some pizza stones to put inside the barbecue and a large flat wooden board to make the pizzas on, otherwise they fall apart when you lift them. The work happens before guests arrive – make a tomato sauce and chop and place every topping you can dream of eating on a pizza in small bowls just ready to be chosen. Everything just tastes better outside, it is really true ... it must be the air or maybe the homemade touch.

DON'T YOU JUST FEEL LIKE JUMPING INTO THESE PICTURES ... HAPPY MEMORIES ARE SOMETIMES ALMOST TANGIBLE. EVEN FROM A FEW PHOTOS YOU CAN FEEL THE LOVELINESS

Left Ohhhhh – those summer nights. When I look at this image I can almost feel the atmosphere and I long for summer to come back. Everything and everybody looks even more beautiful at dusk.

Opposite Finger food ... I like to use a pair of scissors to slice pizzas with, it works really well.

HAPPY HOME MAKE!

PIZZA RECIPE

This will make enough dough for 6 pizzas so just mulitply by however much you need.

YOU WILL NEED

* 650g (1 lb) strong white (bread) flour
* 7g (3 oz) sachet easy-blend yeast
* 2 tsp salt
* 25ml (1 fl oz) olive oil
* 365ml (13 fl oz) warm water

HOW TO MAKE

Mix the flour, yeast and salt in a large bowl and stir in the olive oil. Slowly add the water, mixing to form a soft dough. Knead for 10 minutes. Cover with a cloth and leave to rise for 2 hours. Knead again and shape into balls ready for your guests to roll out.

LET THERE BE LIGHT ...

There is something enchanting about candles, lanterns and lights. Inside or outside, I love the atmosphere of **cosiness** *they bring along. Mix and match every* **shape, colour** *and* **material** *and just light up. Whenever I am in Paris, I am always in awe at the lighting. The* **French** *are so good at lighting their buildings; they instinctively know how to cast just the right shadow. Spend time on your lighting outside, be it* **candles***, bonfire pits or* **electric lights***. It makes everything and everyone look more* **amazing** *and relax a bit more ... and perhaps linger longer at your party.*

BEAUTIFUL BLOCK CANDLES ARE GREAT TO LOOK AT AND EASY TO DECORATE WITH A BIT OF CANDLE PAINT

LAMPSHADE
WITH BIRDS

We hung a glass tealight holder at the centre of this decorated shade. Just make sure the glass is well away from any flammable material.

YOU WILL NEED
* an old lampshade
* long strips of fabric
* birds on clips
* tealight holder and wire

HOW TO MAKE
We stripped a large second-hand lampshade, keeping just a bit of the original lace at the bottom. Tear long fabric strips – 3-4cm (1-1½ inches) wide – and wrap them tightly around the frame. Finally, add birds on clips ... as many as you like.

CANDLES ARE ALWAYS A GOOD IDEA – THEY JUST ADD THAT LITTLE EXTRA CHARM TO THE SETTING – WHILE METAL BOWLS FOR FIREWOOD CREATE WARMTH IN EVERY WAY

POP-UP PEA PICNIC

I am in love with the idea of pop-up events – meaning events that take place in unexpected places for a very limited period of time. It's lovely to be a part of something special and everyone seems to be more open and curious – much more than when you go to a normal restaurant. This green pea picnic is also something you could organize – perhaps you can team up with a few friends and split the work between you. Find a theme and choose the menu – something that can be prepared in advance or barbecued. Organize all the practical things – location, barbecues if necessary, tables, etc. Spend some time decorating, if you can, so it looks welcoming for your guests. Work out the price for one evening or just ask everyone to bring their own drinks, and just charge for the food.

This page Our theme was green peas – quite funny and summery – and above all very, very colourful. Cooking and dining in colours according to seasonal produce is a great way to live in the now.

Bon Appétit!

Bon Appétit!

Clockwise from top left
Cool drinks are always a priority.

Since we have access to lots of cushions and blankets we just filled up a car – if you do not have this you can easily ask everyone to also bring their own blankets and cushions. No one will mind. Everyone is a bit different when sitting close to the ground. I like it.

Let's go green ... summer cabbage with peas, vegetable purée with bacon and peas. Peas on earth ...

PEA BRUSCHETTA

*Easy peasy ... enjoy this green snack,
healthy, colourful and tasty.*

YOU WILL NEED
* 200g (8 oz) frozen peas
* 2 tbsp olive oil
* 8 slices of bread
* 1 clove of garlic
* 200g (8 oz) ricotta cheese
* 50g (2 oz) salad leaves
* salt and freshly ground pepper

HOW TO MAKE
Thaw the peas. Mix with the olive oil and
blend to a fine purée. Season with salt
and pepper. Toast the slices of bread and
rub them with the garlic clove. Cover the
bread generously with the ricotta cheese
and place the pea purée and the salad on
top. Sprinkle with pepper and more salt
if needed. .

TEA FOR TWO

Following on from our pea green picnic, sometimes it can be amusing to do a themed dinner at home. It can be based around a certain ingredient or a colour. We used to live in the countryside and once I created a yellow night – we lived surrounded by fields and every seven years the crops were yellow. This particular summer we were blessed to be surrounded by bright yellow rapeseed fields. I decided to throw a yellow party – I used only yellow plates and cups, made drinks and composed a dinner only in yellow. I can't remember exactly what I made but it was something like vodka and orange juice to drink, eggs mayo, fish with curry and some turmeric rice, and for dessert lemon mousse. Some people even showed up in yellow – and I will always remember that night. It was no more effort than any other dinner party, just more memorable and special.

You can theme up any colours you feel like – here we decided to do a red-and-white special date for two. How welcome would you feel if you were invited to that table? If you start searching high and low inside your kitchen and around the house, you will probably find a lot of things that have the colours you have chosen in them. Over time we sometimes forget to notice what we really have ... and then when we focus our eyes and brains in a different way, it becomes quite a sport to colour track.

Left When doing a colour-themed meal, it is fun to collect and gather items from all over your house and garden and add them into your table setting.

My grandmother was the best hostess I have ever met – she really knew how to make you feel welcome. She would prepare everything for days before your arrival. Nothing was left to coincidence – every detail was timed and calculated so you had better arrive on the dot or hell would break loose. Once you were at her apartment she was ready to give you her full attention. The drinks table was organized so she did not have to get up, the starter was already on the dinner table and the main course in the oven. I still miss her and would love to go for dinner at her place one more time. Perhaps I get my eye for detail from her.

Opposite What a fun feeling you get from this 'make you feel welcome' styling. Now you can serve something as simple as a tomato and mozzarella salad and still look your friend in the eye.

Below A red dinosaur on my plate ... well why not? It will surely put a smile on your face and that is the plan.

Above Grab a cushion from inside your house that matches the chosen colour theme – you will be surprised how many things you have in that particular colour as soon as you start focusing on it. Red is really not a colour I think I have a lot of in my house, but when I went hunting for red I ended up finding quite a lot of things.

Left This cherry garland is hand crocheted. I am sure some of you clever people can make this kind of thing. I myself can only say – not in a million years. I just love looking at mine, handmade by the lovely women of Madagascar.

DRESS UP YOUR TABLE

Take your old candleholders and give them a sweet **makeover** *– you can use* **ribbons**, **paper flowers** *or anything you have ... we all need a new summer dress from time to time. It really doesn't take much, but it is the small details that make the bigger picture. At various flea markets you can often find beautiful teacups – with the most intricate* **prints**, **patterns** *and* **hand-painted details** *on. My grandmother had lots of them. I never really knew what to use them for, and then the lovely idea shown overleaf came up – use them as* **place cards** *and vases at the same time. What*

PUT COLOURFUL STICKERS ON YOUR TABLE – IT WORKS WONDERS AND YOU HAVE NO TABLECLOTH TO WASH AFTERWARDS

CANDLEHOLDERS

If you have some old candleholders that you feel are a bit outdated or boring to look at, this is an easy makeover.

YOU WILL NEED
* candleholders in dire need of upgrading
* paper flowers
* ribbons
* a porcelain or plastic bird
* glitter

HOW TO MAKE
Take some of your favourite candle-holders and wrap them with paper flowers and some ribbons, too, if you like. A bird covered with glitter is a nice piece of decoration, too.

HAPPY HOME
MAKE!

a lovely way to decorate each place setting and take care of your **flower arrangements** *at the same time. Never underestimate the importance of making your guests feel* **welcome**. *If you arrive at a table set with so much love and attention to detail you will for sure straighten your back a bit, be just that little bit* **happier** - *more open and talkative. That is my theory anyway. Good old karma ... make things with love and love comes back at you.*

TEACUP PLACE CARDS

These are so pretty and you can have lots of fun hunting out different mismatched cups.

YOU WILL NEED
* 1 cup per person
* manila labels
* ribbon
* big flower heads

HOW TO MAKE
Find some tiny vintage teacups or espresso cups in flea markets. Tie a small manila label, with name added, to each handle with ribbon. Then place a flower head in each cup, with a little water added in the bottom to keep the flower fresh.

AS CLEAR AS CAN BE – THIS IS ONE BEAUTIFUL TABLE ...

Elisa

Fiona

A WHITE PLATE CAN HELP ENHANCE ALL THE OTHER COLOURS HAPPENING AROUND THIS PLACE SETTING, WHILE STILL CREATING A CALM IMPRESSION

AROUND THE FIRE

There is something utterly fascinating about the elements – one can stare at the ocean for hours, look into fire for an eternity. Just get lost in thought and no thoughts at all. I have great memories of fireplaces – both the woodstove inside the house and around the bonfire outside. A great use for the bonfire is to host a crepe evening – you can buy long-handled pans to use over the fire in any good camping shop. Make the crepes and the filling in advance and just reheat them or, if you have plenty of time on hand, bake them all on site. Throw in a bit of alcohol – mostly for the dramatic effect and the 'woooo' sounds, but also for the taste – ice cream and some fruit compôte and heaven is near.

Below We have a fireplace in our garden as well as one indoors– we actually just dug a hole in the ground, thinking it would make it less sensitive to the wind. I am not sure if it works, but it looks good.

BONFIRE STOOLS

A nice and easy update of the classic rustic bonfire seating.

YOU WILL NEED
* sturdy logs big enough to sit on
* a selection of wood paint

HOW TO MAKE
Paint the top of big logs in an assortment of bright colours and place them around the bonfire. The colours are fun and the paint serves the practical purpose of protecting the tops of the logs so they will last longer.

PROLONGING THE OUTDOOR LIFE

I love the idea of doing things with friends – and not only in summertime. A very cosy way to stay outside even when temperatures go down is to build your event around a big bonfire. In Denmark many parks and forests have large bonfire spots and if you want to organize a fun gathering in autumn you could create an event around mushrooms and mushroom picking. (When it comes to mushroom picking you really need to know what you are doing so you avoid any harmful mushrooms!) Or you could also organize a long forest walk and then finish off around the fire – making bread on a stick and roasting mushrooms. You need to prepare a bit beforehand – bring plates, knives, and forks, and also prepare a simple bread dough just ready to be rolled around sticks and baked over the fire.

Right Gather a stick for each person and remove the bark for about 25cm (10 inches) so you get a nice clean branch to roll the dough around.

Below left and left Shape a piece of dough into a large snake and roll it around a stick. Once the bread is baked and starts smelling really tasty, you can slide it off the stick and put in a bit of butter and jam … very, very nice.

Below Keep the sticks away from the flames, but close enough to the heat so you bake the bread all the way through without burning it. When it is ready to eat, it is easy to slide off without leaving any dough on the stick.

BAKED APPLES

YOU WILL NEED
* 4 apples
* 100g (4 oz) chocolate, chopped
* a handful of raisins and some chopped nuts
* 4 slices of marzipan
* tinfoil

HOW TO MAKE
Use a spoon to remove the apple cores, then fill the hollowed apples with the other ingredients. Wrap the filled apples in tinfoil, put them into the fire and bake for about 10 minutes – but keep an eye on them so they don't burn. Turn the parcels every now and then. The warm apples are best eaten with a spoon or a fork.

Opposite You can almost smell the loveliness of these apples cooked in the fire.

Right A natural way of treasure hunting – the thrill of finding the right and tasty mushrooms is amazing.

Below Chop, chop, chop ... it is that simple. Just throw everything into the pan and after a few minutes you are ready to enjoy the harvest of the day.

IF YOU HAVE
SPENT HOURS
HUNTING
MUSHROOMS
THEY TASTE EVEN
BETTER THAN YOU
CAN IMAGINE –
IF YOU DON'T
HAVE TIME
FOR THIS YOU
CAN ALWAYS
USE MIXED
MUSHROOMS
FROM YOUR
LOCAL GROCERY
STORE

Left As simple as can be ... mushrooms, fresh herbs, garlic, onion, salt and pepper and a great fire. With a good pan happiness is there on a plate.

MUSHROOM RECIPE

Either collect or buy 3 to 4 different kinds of local and seasonal mushrooms.

YOU WILL NEED

* 800g (2 lb) mixed mushrooms
* 2 onions, chopped
* 2 shallots, chopped
* 3 cloves of garlic, chopped
* chives, chopped
* coriander (cilantro), chopped
* salt and pepper
* olive oil
* a dash of cream (optional)

HOW TO MAKE

Fry the onions, shallots and garlic in olive oil until golden – make sure the fire is really hot. Then throw in the mushrooms and stir-fry quickly. Add the herbs at the end and perhaps a bit of cream ... it just makes it even more delicious. Be generous with salt and pepper and enjoy.

PLAYING
OUTDOORS

'Let's stay playful' was one of the slogans
in our collection a few years back, and
this mantra has stuck. I know in my
heart that on the days I wake up with a
playful attitude to life things tend to be
lots more fun. When gathering people
of all ages I feel that something really
valuable happens; the meeting between
young and old, teens and toddlers is very
special. And if you decide to do an activity
together it helps create a very strong
bond and a really light atmosphere.

Previous page Water toys are
always a great idea, for big and
small – they can provide hours of
fun and relaxation in the pool.

Opposite A fabric tipi – quick to
assemble and easy to get in and out
of – is a super space for smaller kids.
Many plans of world domination or
dreams of great romance have been
concocted inside such fabric walls.

PARTYING FOR KIDS

Children are usually very easy to please – especially smaller children. They might not appreciate the beauty of the colour-coordinated set-up so bear in mind that that part you are mostly doing for yourself. But food and fun games is where you make a difference. Be playful – be silly – go overboard on whoopee cushions and funny fake teeth. Being outside for a kids' party has its major perks: no stains, no worries about things being spilled. Decorate with toys and garlands, and adapt the tables and chairs and the games to the age group you are catering for. Only use things you are not worried about losing or breaking – grandmother's fine china is not ideal. I love to use melamine for children – and for adults. It is practically unbreakable and it is fun to eat from. Building up a kid's world makes you want to be a kid again …

Opposite Find appropriate-sized furniture – kids love to play around a table that is just the right height and gives plenty of space to walk around.

This page Use melamine – easy and unbreakable, colourful and fun. Whoopee cushions, fake teeth, soap bubbles and balloons are fun – even for adults – but you must also remember to leave time for chidren to just play freely.

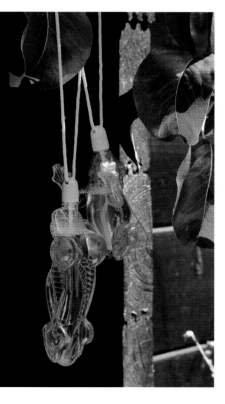

Opposite Practical, fun, colourful and playful – that is always a good start when organizing any party, and especially one for kids.

This page It could be fun to organize a kids' party for adults as well with all the same props and toys ... I think I will do that soon.

Stay Playful...

FOR YOU!

NIKLAS

ALL STRUNG UP

I don't know about you guys, but every time we host a party tons and tons of glasses are used. In order to avoid this, or to at least perhaps limit the amount of glasses a tiny bit, make a glass for each guest with their name on it. It makes you feel so very welcome to have one waiting for you ...

YOU WILL NEED
* assorted stickers and a pen
* washing line or string
* pegs (pins) and clips

HOW TO MAKE
Make a cup for each guest with a name tag and other decorations, then hang them up.

GO ALL IN ON PAPER GARLANDS AND COLOURFUL DECORATIONS – THEY CAN SMARTEN UP ANY ROOM OR SPACE IN A FEW MINUTES

Left Meet you in the bamboo bar ... I bought this bar many years ago and we have used it so much, and lent it to friends for their parties as well. You can do that too – put together a party kit with cups, plates, lanterns, a bar, a few tall tables. Invest together with a group of friends and everyone can just borrow it whenever needed.

Opposite Sometimes it is great to invest a bit of time in organizing a special set-up for a special occasion – a huge pink cake like this one ordered at the baker creates memories that will never be forgotten.

MEMORY GAME

It's fun to play memory games – even if it can be rather frustrating when that five-year-old beats you every time ... What I love about this is that you can use the cards as coasters and then afterwards as a memory game.

YOU WILL NEED
* pressed flowers and leaves
* patterned paper – double up on one specific pattern
* glue stick
* laminating machine and sleeves

HOW TO MAKE
Press flowers and leaves from your garden. Make sure to have 2 almost identical of each. Cut circles from lovely patterned paper. Glue the circles together – all upper sides should be from the same paper pattern. Glue the flowers and leaves on to the other side of the circles. Laminate them and carefully cut out the circles with a 5mm ($^1/_{16}$ inch) border so they don't fall apart.

HAPPY HOME
MAKE!

This page Curling up on a soft couch to watch a feel-good movie ... happy moments.

MOVIE MAGIC

I always find outdoor cinemas very romantic. Often you see them in movies as part of small town functions where everybody sits on the grass, having picnics, holding hands and just enjoying the beauty of a nice movie in special surroundings. And there really is something magical about watching a movie under stars. It is a special experience and the memory will stay very strong, making it something to look forward to when winter lasts a bit too long and it is too cold for late-night outdoor activities.

We happen to have a big white wall in our garden and one summer a few years ago a friend of ours suggested this could make a great screen for a movie. With the help of technically minded friends, a few loudspeakers, a laptop and a small projector we were up and running. These movie nights rank in my top five of absolute favourite evening things to do ...

Above Some of my best summer memories are these outdoor cinema nights. We pull together every piece of furniture, every mattress and every cushion we have, and prepare a lovely soft spot for each guest.

Left Last summer we had a lot of teenagers who decided to spend the whole night sleeping outside – just the way I love my house and garden to be used and lived in.

Opposite Prepare plenty of blankets for when the temperature starts to drop. Delegate the tasks so everyone does something – someone in charge of snacks, popcorn, drinks, etc. And another in charge of the technical set-up so you are ready to show the movie when darkness falls.

TIPI - TEE HEE!

Large tipis have this dreamy fantasy feel about them – you almost make yourself believe you are a Native American squaw ready to dance around the totem pole at any moment. What is great about them is the fact that you can stand up inside, walk around and in the very large ones you can even have a fireplace in the middle ... and feel like you are part of a Disney movie. Big campsites and some nature parks even have tipis for rent. This tipi is for kids; it is very easy to set up, and equally easy to move around. I am sure children will have a wonderful time running in and out of this little sanctuary all day long or sitting with the tent openings firmly closed dreaming up their own magic world. I remember the joy my own kids could have just with a large cardboard box, crawling inside and out for hours ...

Opposite A tipi is easy to set up, and can be placed inside or outside – at least when it is a relatively small size. But oh to be a child and spend all day playing inside and out of this lovely world ... who should be so lucky?

Above and left There is a small crocheted garland to decorate the tipi and nice bags to keep your snacks safely stored – beauty is in the details.

GREAT PLAYERS
NEED TO STOCK
UP ON FOOD AND
DRINKS REGULARLY,
SO WHEN ENERGY
LEVELS DIP
BE READY WITH
SNACKS AND TREATS

Left and opposite A few masks and props set a theme – everyone is always someone else when putting on a mask. Or when taking it off …

JAM SESSION

Many of us seem to be caught up in such busy lives we sometimes don't have time to see each other. And when we do, then only to eat and drink and drink some more. Don't get me wrong, I am a fan of that. But really, I love the idea of *doing* things together, walking, cooking, baking, playing, exercising. Gatherings are a growing trend – at least I hope so, and I will do my part to spread the idea. You can invite friends over to make soup or meat sauce – anything really. You chop and cook and chat and laugh, and then when everyone leaves they take something with them – meat sauce for the freezer, perhaps. Wouldn't you love to receive a meal for four – prepared by your friend – to put in your freezer and to pull it out on a day you do not feel like cooking? I would be thrilled, both to be the cook who gives this present or to receive and enjoy it.

Opposite and overleaf Invite a few people over and make a small plan of action as to who brings what: jars, stickers, glitter, pens, plus ingredients for whatever you wish to make, such as chutneys, syrups or jams. If the weather allows you can work outside – cutting and pitting fruit is much more fun when in good company and the mess doesn't matter as much outdoors. Once you have made the preserves, you can start decorating jars. At the end of the day you share the produce between you, and everyone leaves with a great mix of jams and chutneys to take home.

PLUM 'N' CINNAMON CHUTNEY

This could be for your own store cupboard or be presented as a gift.

YOU WILL NEED
* 1kg (2 lb) plums, halved and pitted
* 5 cinnamon sticks
* 4 onions, coarsely chopped
* 200ml vinegar
* 300g (10 oz) sugar
* 1 tbsp cornflour (cornstarch)
* 1 tbsp water

HOW TO MAKE
Roughly chop half the plums and set aside. Dry-fry the cinnamon sticks in a heavy-based pan for a few minutes over a low heat. Add the onions, vinegar, sugar and the halved plums and simmer for 30 minutes until the plums are tender. Dissolve the cornflour (cornstarch) in the water and add to the chutney, stirring constantly. Bring to the boil, add the remaining chopped plums and simmer for 10 minutes. Pour the chutney into sterilized jars and tighten the lids thoroughly. Store in a cool place.

TO BE CREATIVE TOGETHER IS ALMOST LIKE MEDITATING. WHEN YOU FOCUS ON CRAFTING YOU ARE TOGETHER IN A DIFFERENT WAY – SOMETIMES YOU CHAT AND TALK, OTHER MOMENTS YOU JUST ENJOY SILENTLY

Above All the necessities for an afternoon full of fun and craftmaking. This is fun for both kids and adults. Use pens and draw faces on the chestnuts or string them on a wire for a lovely wreath to hang on your front door.

Opposite This couple is one cute pair – I would love to have them over for drinks and dinner anytime, and perhaps a bit of dancing afterwards. A nice autumn walk is the first thing to organize, for hunting and gathering.

CELEBRATING AUTUMN

When the summer heydays are over, there's still plenty of outside fun to be had. There is no need to cut the outdoor season short just because it gets a bit chillier. Autumn calls for chestnut and acorn gathering. And leaves … lots of beautiful leaves. After enjoying a day in the brisk autumn weather it is time for an afternoon of fun getting crafty with the loot of the day. All kids love this, making animals and people with matchstick legs and acorn hats. Use pens or crayons to draw faces on the chestnuts. You can create entire worlds inhabited by these lovely creatures. Or you can dip acorns in glue and glitter for Christmas decorations. And if you are lucky enough to have foraged edible chestnuts, hurry up and put them in the oven. Serve with butter and salt – a simple, but oh so delicious, snack.

Opposite An autumn garland in the making. I love the toned-down colour palette, which gets a hit of orange and bright green from the leaves and woolly pompons.

Right Bring the outside in on your window-sill by incorporating nature's elements in your decorating. Create garlands with a clear autumn theme. Tie leaves on a vase or bottle for a quick seasonal upgrade.

WHEN AUTUMN DAYS ARE HERE MAKE THE MOST OF WHAT THEY HAVE TO OFFER. LIVE IN THE MOMENT, ENJOYING THE SEASON

PLAY TOGETHER STAY TOGETHER

*There are many ways to stay **playful** and active. Playing ball and ring-tossing games can really **activate** your playful side and your social skills. And exercise is great for people of all ages. I never dreamed that a punch bag and a pair of **boxing gloves** could make my heart sing, but it is so much fun to box – a really fantastic way to get your pulse up and your frustrations out. I forget everything around me and just feel like*

METAL SHELVES THAT CAN STAY OUTDOORS MAKE IT EASY TO STAY PLAYFUL – ACCESSIBILITY, ACCESSIBILITY, ACCESSIBILITY ...

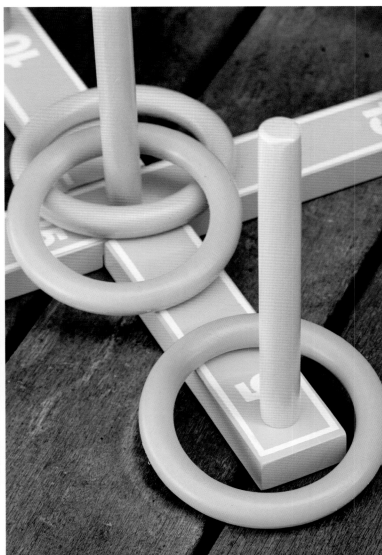

*I am Muhammad Ali. A punchbag is the biggest investment here. If you want to create a small **cross training** path in your garden you can buy a few kettlebells (great for muscular strength training) and a **skipping rope** (super for cardio rate and also fun – it makes you feel like a young girl in the schoolyard again). If you buy an old tractor tyre you can flip it around on a small area and activate lots of muscles. I of course prefer it to be painted in a nice **pink** colour ... If you are a group of **friends** planning to work out together it is a good idea to find a personal trainer who can come and show you the right way to get **started**.*

I HAVE RECENTLY FOUND A PASSION FOR BOXING – BELIEVE ME IT HAS TAKEN ME BY SURPRISE TOO. GIVE IT A TRY. IT'S SUCH A FUN WAY TO GET RID OF STRESS AND AGGRESSION AND BE SPORTY AT THE SAME TIME

BOXING WITH SOMEONE INTO THE PADS IS ALMOST AS GREAT FUN AS DANCING

MOVEABLE SPACES

Road trips are fairy-tale moments – they can be short or long, it doesn't matter. You don't need to take a six-month sabbatical to cross America – even if that is undeniably an amazing experience. Just get beyond your garden and go for even more outdoorsy adventures. Enjoy the freedom to just pack your things and go! If it is only for one night or a weekend trip to the coast in your camper van it can still be an adventure. Stop and enjoy the little things, count the butterflies and dream about the clouds ...

Previous page A home on wheels. To be free as a bird, and yet in the comfort of your own bed ... the best of both worlds for me.

Opposite Look at your caravan and see if there are any possibilities you have missed or just not utilized yet. For example, install a few small shelves in the door to store kitchen and cleaning items.

COOL CARAVAN

Oh, the freedom of just grabbing your keys and going wherever the mood takes you, even if it is only for one night. If you have a caravan you have an extra home on wheels. I am a huge fan of the Danish author Karen Blixen (1885–1962) and her sense of beauty and the adventurous life she lived in Africa for many years. When I watch the movie about the part of her life where she lived in Kenya – *Out of Africa* – I just want to jump into the movie and be part of the scenery. She did a lot of

Left and above The almost modern version of Karen Blixen's *Out of Africa* ... all we need now is Denys Finch Hatton.

Below Everyday magic – so easy to create with just a few colourful cups and some cheerful cushions.

safaris in Africa, always in great style. Whenever we go camping, I think of her, and try to create my own version of a beautiful scenery. No lions involved though ...

Remember that compact living doesn't mean compromising on style. Bring with you all your favourite tableware, best cushions, softest quilts and comfiest outdoor chairs. With a few clever storage solutions you can really fill up your caravan and never end up with a messy look. Spending the entire summer holiday like this is something we have always enjoyed as a family.

A NICE CUP OF
TEA, A SUMMER
DRESS AND
SOME FUNKY
MUSIC ...
YES, PLEASE –
ANYTIME

Right A few props and you
have a universe at your
fingertips ... all the makings
of a moveable feast.

READY FOR ADVENTURE

When you are the lucky owner of a van like this you are also the beneficiary of lots of waves, smiles and words from people you meet on the road. This caravan is actually my wedding ring. When this wonderful van came up for sale, I begged my husband to buy it instead of a ring. Since then my family and I have enjoyed many weekends and summer holidays in it. It is amazing what you can find room for in a small space and still keep it neat, if you put your mind to it. When our kids were little we used to go camping in this van only 4km (2½ miles) away from our home. If you asked my children what was the best holiday ever they would always answer camping – and they are well-travelled globetrotter kids who have been to some pretty amazing places all around the world. I am only saying this to tell you that awesome adventures have nothing to do with how far away you

Opposite and below One day by a lake, the next in the woods; perhaps we will go into the mountains tomorrow? The joy of being footloose and fancy free.

Right A blue fridge – always a good companion. A multicolored string of lights adds that final festive touch to the setting. Colour the world and yourself happy.

Opposite Make sure to pack lots of entertainment for the kids, such as inflatable beach stuff. Frisbees and tennis rackets are always fun and they hardly take up any room.

Right Bright and bold – if you have a neutral background it is easy to change the look of the space just with a few blankets. You can tone up or down on colours according to your mood.

USE LOTS OF BASKETS AND BOXES TO HAVE AND TO HOLD EVERYTHING YOU NEED FOR A FUN ROAD TRIP

go or how exotic the places are you visit. A caravan is truly an extension of your own home. You can bring all your favourite items that you just can't live without, as well as everything necessary for a fabulous time. It is all about organizing your stuff and using clever storage solutions to keep it neat. When it comes to setting up camp on back roads and rest areas, make sure to check the rules with the local authorities. Not every country permits camping outside designated camping areas. But if they do, just remember one rule – leave nothing but your footprints. Make sure to take all your rubbish and other belongings with you.

TEA TOWEL CURTAIN

A curtain made with a tea (dish) towel and a few clips – that is truly my kind of curtain.

YOU WILL NEED
* string and hooks
* clothes pegs (pins)
* a tea (dish) towel

HOW TO MAKE
Fasten the string to 2 hooks and simply attach the tea towel with pegs (pins).

GOOD TO GO

*When we lived in Paris and we had no terrace or garden I became the master of picnics in nearby parks. At the time I did not have **melamine** in my life so I carried my beautiful Tricia Guild plates around. They looked **amazing** but there was always a high breakage risk ... Now I have a big pile of portable tableware – hard to break, easy to carry, colourful as ever – and I **love** it. I use it always - **inside and out** – and each time I look at a piece I feel happy inside. Do not ask me to choose a favourite ... I love each and every one of them.*

I ALWAYS GET INSPIRED BY RANDOM
COLOUR-STACKING COMBINATIONS

RICE STOCKISTS

Follow us around the world:

rice_up

ricedk
charlotte_rice

Selected stockists with RICE
products. Visit www.rice.dk
for inspiration.

AUSTRALIA
Corner Store
147 South Terrace
(cnr Price St)
Fremantle WA 6160
0061 8 9336 3005
www.cornerstore.net.au

Corner Store
201-205 Stirling Highway
(cnr Loch St)
Claremont WA 6010
0061 9286 2280
www.cornerstore.net.au

Corner Store
25 Market Street
Fremantle WA 6160
0061 9336 3010
www.cornerstore.net.au

Corner Store
649F Beaufort Street
(next to Dome)
Mount Lawley 6050
0061 8 9228 1222
www.cornerstore.net.au

Lark Store
30 Armstrong Street North
Ballarat VIC 3350
0061 3 466 400 219
www.larkstore.com.au

AUSTRIA
Blumen Thell
Obere Hauptstraße 39
7121 Weiden am See
0043 2167 40158
www.blumenthell.at

Ediths
Hauptstraße 21a
6840 Götzis
0043 5523 56777
www.ediths.at

BRAZIL
Coisas da Doris
Al. Ministro Rocha Azeve. 834
01410-002 Sao Paulo
0055 11 308 319 62

CHINA
Motherswork
L-VDM-20, Level 1
SOLANA Shopping Mall
No. 6 Chaoyang Park Road
Beijing 100125
0086 188 1086 2900
www.motherswork.cn

DENMARK
Continental
St. Sct. Peder Stræde 5
8800 Viborg
0045 86 61 43 24

Forvandlingskuglen
Skånegade 7
2300 København S
0045 36 30 66 66

Hesselholt
Hulsigvej 19
9990 Skagen
0045 98 44 64 42
www.galleri-hesselholt.dk

Invi2
Strandvejen 456
6854 Henne Strand
0045 7525 5060
www.invi2.dk

Lirum Larum Leg
Engholmvej 16
3100 Hornbæk
0045 70 26 98 90
www.lirumlarumleg.dk

Mandrup Poulsen Tapeter
Rantzausgade 1B
9000 Ålborg
0045 9625 8505

Pang Christianshavn
Sankt Annæ gade 31
1416 København K
0045 32 96 68 00
www.pangchristianshavn.dk

Pure Style Living
www.purestyleliving.dk

Rum9
Storegade 19, 4780 Stege
0045 40 96 86 32
www.rum9.dk

FRANCE
Loulou Addict
25, rue Keller
75011 Paris
0033 01 49 29 00 61
www.loulouaddict.com

Le Panier D'Eglantine
6, Grande rue
54000 Nancy
0033 3 83 20 61 47
www.lepanierdeglantine.com

Trait d'union
22, place Portalis
83270 Saint Cyr sur mer
0033 4 94 26 24 78

Zazou
4, rue du Colonel Picot
29200 Brest
0033 2 98 46 21 90
www.zazou-boutique.fr

GERMANY
Danish Homestyle
An der Reitbahn 3
21218 Seevetal
0049 4105 556055
www.danish-homestyle.de

Das Tropenhaus
www.das-tropenhaus.de

Format Essen
Rüttenscheider Strasse 137
45130 Essen
0049 201 87423627

Geliebtes Zuhause
www.geliebtes-zuhause.de

Grüner Krebs
Erbprinzenstr. 21
76133 Karlsruhe
0049 721 25 542
www.gruenerkrebs.de

Kontrast GmbH
Hanauer Landstrasse 297
60314 Frankfurt am Main
0049 69 90 439 30
www.kontrastmoebel.de

Korbmayer
Schulstr. 2
70173 Stuttgart
0049 711 2298110
www.korbmayer.de

Max.Leben
Untermarkt 17
82515 Wolfratshausen
0049 8171481048
www.max-leben.de

Michaelsen Scandinavian Living
Hüxstrasse 62
23552 Lübeck
0049 451 88998020
www.michaelsen-living.de

Mohren-Haus
Obere Brücke 14
96047 Bamberg
0049 951 980 380
www.mohren-haus.de

Nostalgie im Kinderzimmer
www.nostalgieimkinderzimmer.de

Sylter Wohnlust
Silwai 5
25980 Sylt
0049 4651 98380
www.sylter-wohnlust.de

HONG KONG
Mirth Home
The Mezzanine Floor, Yip Kan St.
Wong Chuk Hang
00852 25539811
www.mirthhome.com

IRELAND
Avoca
11-13 Suffolk Street
Dublin 2
00353 16774215
www.avoca.ie

Avoca
Rathcoole, Fitzmaurice
N7 Naas Road
Dublin
00353 12571800
www.avoca.ie

Avoca
The Mill at Avoca Village
Co. Wicklow
00353 40235105
www.avoca.ie Ireland

Avoca
Kilmacanogue, Bray
Co. Wicklow
00353 12867466
www.avoca.ie

Avoca
Letterfrack, Connemara
Co. Galway
00353 9541058
www.avoca.ie

Avoca
Moll's Gap, Kenmare
Co. Kerry 00353 6434720
www.avoca.ie

The Garden Pavilion
Myrtle Hill
Ballygarvan
Co. Cork
00353 214888134
www.thepavilion.ie

ISRAEL
Sofi
3 Nakhman st. Shuk
Pishpeshim
68138 Tel Aviv
00972 35162077

ITALY
Dulcamara
Via Mayer 54 / 56
57125 Livorno (LI)
0039 0586891607

Gallina Smilza
Via S. Stefano 14 d
40125 Bologna
0039 0515870640
www.gallinasmilza.it

Mack
Via Ugo Foscolo 61
30017 Jesolo (VE)
0039 0421375219

Mezzanotte Co. Ltd
Viale Premuda 13
20129 Milano
0039 0236586288
www.mezzanottestore.it

JAPAN
Ann A.
5557-124 Mukojima-cho
Onomichi-shi
Hiroshima 722-0073
www.monoanna.exblog.jp

Age Life
1661-1 Kaku Nakatsu-shi Oita
Oita 871-0152
0081 979-53-8808

Momo Shop
2-12-30 Higashikaigankita
Chigasaki-shi
Kanagawa 253-0053
0081 467-83-2424
www.momoshop.jp

MEXICO
**El Palacio de Hierro
Coyoacán**
Centro Coyoacán
Av. Coyoacán No. 2000
Col. Xoco C.P
03330 México D.F
0052 5422-1900
www.elpalaciodehierro.com

**El Palacio de Hierro
Durango**
Durango No. 230
Col. Roma Norte C.P
06700 México D.F
0052 5242-9000
www.elpalaciodehierro.com

El Palacio de Hierro Santa Fe
Vasco de Quiroga No. 3800
Col. Vista Hermosa, C.P.
5257-9200
0052 5257-9200
www.elpalaciodehierro.com

NETHERLANDS
Heerlijck Thuis
Grote Kerk Straat 7
5911 CG Venlo
0031 77 3513008
www.heerlijckthuis.nl

Lant van Texsel
Waalderstraat 23
1791 EB Den Burg
0031 22 23 22 031
www.winkeloptexel.nl

Nijhof
Minervaweg 3
3741 GR Baarn
0031 35 5486192
www.nijhofbaarn.nl

Zinin
Burg. Reigerstraat 11
3581 KJ Utrecht 0031
30 2518178
www.zininshop.nl

NORWAY
Britts Boutique
Heiloveien 4, 9015 Tromsø
0047 77607195
www.britts.no

Frk. Fryd
Storveien 84
1624 Gressvik
0047 90 20 20 03

Grønn
Lilleakerveien 31
0283 Oslo
0047 22519700

Hakallegarden
Hakallestranda
6149 Åram
0047 7001588
www.alpakka.no

Rafens
Grensen 16, 0159 Oslo
0047 91745415
www.rafens.no

Ting Bergen
Bryggen 13, 5003 Bergen
0047 55215480
www.tingbutikken.no

Ting Oslo
Akersgata 18
0158 Oslo
0047 22424242
www.tingbutikken.no

Traktøren Bogstadveien
Bogstadveien 25
0355 Oslo
0047 22600808

SINGAPORE
The Childrens Showcase
501, Bukit Timah Road
#02-31/33 Singapore
0065 6474 7440

The Childrens Showcase
200 Turf Club Road
#02-06/K45 Singapore
0065 6474 7440

The Childrens Showcase
Tanglin Mal
#03-08A Singapore
0065 6474 7440

SOUTH KOREA
Brandneo
1F 5-10, Apgujeong-ro 50-gil
Gangnam-gu
135-897 Seoul
0082 23446 6535
www.styliti.com

SPAIN
Suit Beibi
Benet Mateu 52
08034 Barcelona
0034 932057260
www.suitbeibi.com

SWEDEN
Artiklar
Fleminggatan 65
112 32 Stockholm
0046 8 652 93 35
www.artiklarsthlm.se

Boink
www.boinkstore.com

Inreda
www.inreda.com

Milq
Gamla Brogatan 26
Stockholm
0046 8 411 32 50
www.milq.se

R.O.O.M Stockholm
Täby Centrum
106 37 Stockholm
0046 86925000

Slättarps Gård
Rågv.9 23193, Trelleborg
0046 733835995

Style4 Solutions AB
Verkstadsg. 3
59933 Ödeshög
0046 730 27 90 49

Syster Lycklig
Tegnergatan 12
113 58
Stockholm
0046 8 612 65 64
www.systerlycklig.se

Udda Tina
www.uddatina.se

SWITZERLAND
Ademas
Garnmark 1
8400 Winterthur
0041 522122423
www.ademas.ch

Ars Longa
Bahnhofplatz 3
8001 Zürich
0041 44 211 22 02
www.arslonga.ch

The Home Shop
Rain 14
5000 Aarau
0041 628234946
www.thehomeshop.ch

Lieblings
Vordergasse 47
8200 Schaffhausen
0041 52 6201257
www.lieblings.ch

Werkeria
Bahnhofstr. 20
7000 Chur
0041 812504045
www.werkeria.ch

UNITED ARAB EMIRATES
Pantry Cafe
Al Safa
1 Dubai
0097 143883868
www.pantrycafe.me

UK
Burford Garden Center
Shilton Road
Burford OX18 4PA
0044 1993823117
www.burford.co.uk

Cherryade
180 Bridport Road
Poundbury
Dorchester DT1 3BN
0044 1305266400
www.cherryadestore.co.uk

Fig 1
51 St Lukes Road
Bristol BS3 4RX
0044 1173308167
www.fig1.co.uk

Fuego
5A Coombe Street
Lyme Regis
Dorset DT7 3PY
0044 1297 443933
www.fuegoshop.co.uk

Gazebo
74 High Street
Totnes TQ9 5SN
0044 1803 863679
www.whatalovelyshop.co.uk

Indian Summer
624c Fulham Road
Parsons Green
London SW6 5RS
0044 2079374686
www.indiansummershop.com

Oliver Bonas
129 Kensington High Street
London W8 6SU
0044 2077318234
www.oliverbonas.com

The Orchid House
15 Lake Road
Keswick CA12 5BS
0044 1768772875
www.theorchidhouse.net

Sisters Guild
32 Catherine Hill
Frome, Somerset BA11 1BZ
0044 1373471988
www.sistersguild.co.uk

The Whiting Post
The Clothes Horse
58 Harbour Street
Whitstable
Kent CT5 1AG
0044 1227772192
www.thewhitingpost.com

USA
Go Living
1160 Industrial Road, Suite 16
San Carlos
CA 94070 001 6507166010
www.goliving-us.com

Huset
1316 1/2 Abbot Kinney Blvd
Venice, Malibu
CA 90291
001 3104595524
www.huset-shop.com

Originals
261 Sound Beach Avenue, Old
Greenwich
CT 06870
001 2034612290

Shop Sweet Lulu
www.shopsweetlulu.com

Sweet William
85 Kenmare Street
Manhattan New York
NY 10012
001 212 343 7301
www.sweetwilliamltd.com

Sweet William
324 Withe Ave
Brooklyn
NY 11249
001 718 218 6946
www.sweetwilliamltd.com

Sweet William
1406 Micheltorena Street
Los Angeles
CA 90026
001 323 741 8161
www.sweetwilliamltd.com

Yolk
1626 Silverlake Blvd
Los Angeles
CA 90026
001 3236604315

ACKNOWLEDGEMENTS

This is my second *Happy Home* book and my fifth book altogether - I have already written three cookery books in Danish. I do love making books ...

Last summer when we discussed the making of this book I was in a situation where I really did not have the time or the energy available to complete it, but thanks to some very beautiful people close to my heart we made it:

First of all thank you Dagmar Haustrup for making me reconsider the 'no sorry not possible' decision. You were right – it was possible.

To Fiona Hedigan for giving me the mantra 'creativity over chaos' – it saved me and still does.

To Morten Tillitz for keeping me sane and pushing me around on the sporty track, and for inspiring me to have the Play Together Stay Together sporty section in my life and in this book.

To Ane Bilde for carrying out the practical and creative part of most of the DIY projects – you're the best.

To Louise Fechtenborg for jumping in and going from zero to one hundred very fast. To Nikoline Helveg for doing the same thing, helping out just at the right time.

One of the most important people, who makes things happen and always take my crazy ideas to a much better level than I imagined - Thomas Lukasiewicz. Big big thanks.

To Stine from Skovdal & Skovdal, the coolest photographer even on very hot summer days. To Skovdal & Skovdal for a great 'pea picnic' event.

To Mitzi Nielsen for eagle eyes on all words.

To the lovely families who let me into me their homes and gardens: Birgitte Bøegh Sørensen, Susanne Borgaard, Tina Hansen, Inge Fjord, Lisser Nygaard, Jane Wulff, Ane Bilde, Signe Wenneberg and Emil.

Thank to Brian Djernes and Louise Andresen for delivering amazing garden furniture from Cane-Line and Sika-Horsnaes.

To Cathy and the wonderful Le Gallic family for styling help and good looks on one hot summer day and night, and for just fitting in perfectly. Thank you also to my amazingly gorgeous children Max and Selma and their friends for great modelling work.

To the weather gods for playing along so nicely

To Skodsborg Kurhotel for giving me beautiful shelter while putting all words together.

To Will Taylor for writing the foreword. I fell in love with you before we ever met just through your slogan 'because beige is boring'- together we do what we can to colour the world just a tiny bit happier.

To Sian Parkhouse for great editing, and always keeping grounded and on both feet even with a broken ankle.

Last but not least big love and thank you to my family, and especially to Philippe, my rock.

I really hope I haven't forgotten anyone. If I have please grab one of these thank yous and feel free to scream at me next time we meet ...

It was fun.
Charlotte
xoxo

PHOTOGRAPHY CREDITS

All photography is by Skovdal & Skovdal (Stine Christensen www.skovdal.dk) except for the following:

photographs on pages 7, 9, 46, 47, 150, 151 and 184: RICE image bank

photographs on pages 166, 167, 168, 169: Ane Kirstine Bilde, styling and idea / Uffe Bilde, photos / www.alongcameaggie.dk

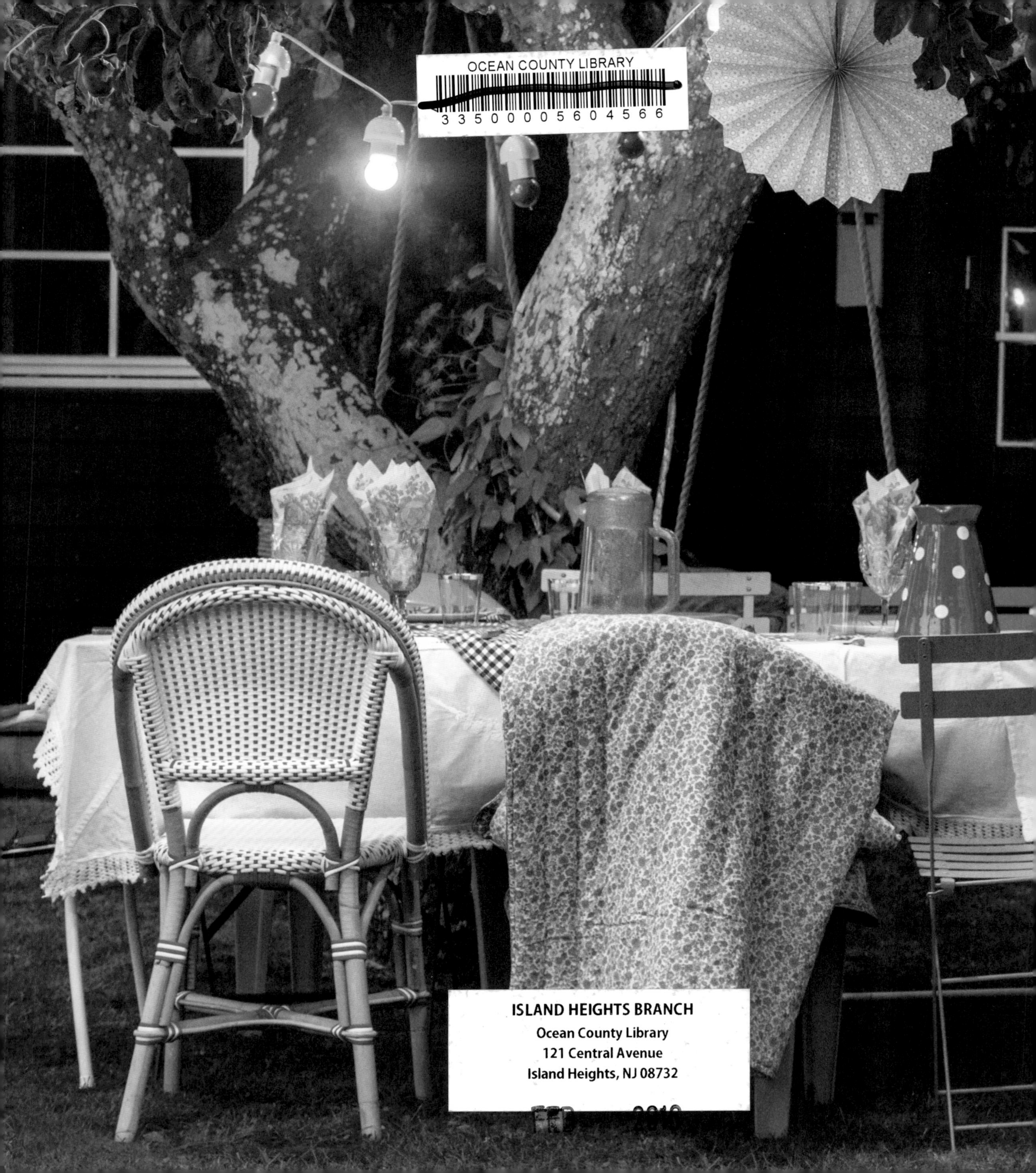